African Birds:

Fun Facts and Fantastic Photos
for Kids!
Learn About African Animals.

by
Sean Liburd

Table of Contents

Introduction

Welcome to *African Birds: Fun Facts and Fantastic Photos for Kids! Learn About African Animals!*

In this book, we will explore and learn all about the species of birds in Africa. Included are fun facts and beautiful pictures of these beautiful birds for better learning.

Find out what they eat, where they go, what they look like, and how they behave. With the help of this book, you will learn the wonders of birds that live far away – in Africa!

Dive in and let us begin learning about the birds of Africa!

Thank you for downloading this book and we hope you have fun learning!

Enjoying Birds

Birds are truly wonderful creatures. They live and fly all around us, but the world of birds is a lot bigger than you think. Did you know that there are 10,000 different species of birds in the world? These are the species that you cannot find at home, in your backyard, in the park, and sometimes not even at the zoo!

What Are Birds?

Did you know that birds have been around for millions of years? In fact, some scientists believe that they are descendants from dinosaurs! The first ever bird was the **archaeopteryx.** Just like birds, it can fly. And just like dinosaurs, it had claws and sharp teeth! But today, they look friendlier than they used to.

Birds in Africa come in all shapes and sizes. There are birds that are bigger than a person and birds that are no bigger than a pea. For people living in other countries, they can plan *birding tours to* Africa so they can enjoy the beauty of African birds.

Understanding Birds

Birds have body parts that are different from humans. Their bodies are special because it allows them to fly. They have powerful muscles and lighter bones, which help birds of flight carry their weight into the air.

Bird Beaks

The beaks or bills of birds are used mainly for eating and catching food. The food that birds eat helps to determine the shape of their beak. For example, **predatory birds** like *hawks* have powerful beaks with pointed tips, which help them catch their prey. Birds that eat insects have long, pointy bills. Lastly, birds that eat mostly fruits and nuts such as *finches* usually have thicker beaks.

Wings

Birds have *wings* that help them fly. They flap their powerful wing muscles and use **thermal lift** or the rising hot air to fly. Not all birds are able to fly. There are some that cannot fly because their bodies are too heavy, but usually they don't need to because everything they need is on the ground.

Bird Habitats in Africa

Birds can have many different homes or *habitats* where they live and raise offspring. Their habitats are where they can naturally be found, meaning that a *zoo* or *bird cage* are not a birds natural habitat. A variety of birds can be found across the continent of Africa.

What are Bird Habitats?

Just like you, birds need homes to live. They need a safe place to build a nest and find food. The African *flamingo* are water birds. They live in the lakes or *lagoons* in Africa because they eat shrimp and algae. There are also the *sociable weavers* that build big nests for their community.

There are around *2,300* different recorded species of birds in Africa while and around 1,800 of these species cannot be found anywhere else! - Too many to fit one book.

Today, the birds of Africa are protected and studied by humans. Some of these birds are **endangered** and it is our responsibility to take care of them.

The Beauty of Colors

The feathers of birds have many colors. If you look outside, you can find a lot of birds with pretty colors. And in Africa, there are a great deal of colorful birds. The *lilac-breasted roller* in South Africa has many bright colors. Some even compare them to rainbows. But did you know that there are meanings behind the colors of birds?

Some male birds have many colors to attract female birds. Scientists also believe that healthy male birds have brighter colors to help them scare off other birds to and protect their **territory.** Other birds have colors that match their surroundings. This is called **camouflage.** If they are harder to see, they can avoid being hunted by predators. And lastly, there are birds that get their color from the food they eat.

Birds and the Seasons

Some birds change the way they behave depending on the season. Most of the time, birds only build nests and lay eggs during a specific season, which can last for months. Some birds even change color depending on the season. For example, the *willow grouse* turns white during the winter. This will make them harder to be seen in the snow.

Breeding Season

The breeding season of birds is when males attract females. After mating, the female bird lays eggs, which will hatch into chicks. Some birds lay one egg while others lay many. This depends on the species of the bird.

A lot of bird species are born *blind* and bald. The chicks will have to be protected by one or both parents to survive. Just like you, chicks need food to grow. A bird parent will also have to bring back food to the nest to feed the chicks. This will happen until the chick is big enough to leave the nest.

A lot of bird species move to warmer places when they breed. Scientists have found yearly patterns of this behavior. This is called **migration.** A popular migrating bird is the *swallow*.

African Ostrich

The **flightless** *ostrich* is popular for being the biggest living species of birds. There is no other bird bigger than the ostrich right now! There were bigger birds in the past like the *Pelagornis sandersi* and the *elephant bird*. Ostriches are native in Africa and run the wide and open *savannas* and *miombos* with their powerful legs. These legs can carry them in speeds of over *70 kilometers per hour* – about twice the speed of the fastest man alive.

White-Headed Buffalo Weaver

Also known as the *white-faced buffalo weaver*, the *white-headed buffalo weaver* is a small bird native to Eastern Africa. As their name suggests, they have white feathers on their heads. They can grow up to 7.5 inches in length and do not have differences in **plumage** between a male and female.

Cape Vulture

The *cape culture,* also known as the *Cape Griffon,* is a large **scavenging** bird that can be found in *South Africa.* They can grow for up to *45 inches* in length. They are not as tall, but their **wingspan** can measure up to *8.5 feet* in length – making them look huge while in flight.

Ground Hornbill

The *ground hornbill* is an odd-looking bird that is native to the southern and eastern parts of Africa. Despite their name, ground hornbills can actually *fly*, but they spend most of their time on the ground. A male Ground Hornbill can grow up to *51 inches long* and weigh up to *6.2 kilograms*.

Grey Crowned Crane

The *grey crowned crane* is a species of birds that commonly **flock** in numbers of *30* up to *150*. They can grow up to *3.3 feet* in height and *3.5 kilograms* in weight. When fully extended, their wingspan can measure up to *2 meters*. The most notable trait of the grey crowned crane is the set of golden feathers on top of its white head that looks like a crown.

African Flamingos

There are different species of *flamingos* scattered throughout the world. The most common *greater flamingo* is located in parts of Europe, Asia, and Africa. In addition to the greater flamingo, Africa is also the home of the *lesser flamingo*. They are notable for their pink plumage, but they are born with grey feathers. They get this color from the shrimp and algae they eat.

Turaco

The *turaco* is a family of birds that includes the *white-cheeked turaco* in the picture above. Their wings are short, but their tails are long. They have **crests** that give them their unique look. Their color is usually blue-green and can grow from *14* to *28 inches*.

Fork-Tailed Drongo

The *fork-tailed* is a small bird that is common in southern Sahara, Africa. They get their name from their fork-shaped tails. These insect-eating birds are only *25 centimeters* long. Despite their small size, these birds are fearless and can fight bigger animals.

Abu Markub

The *abu markub* or *shoebill* is known for its odd bill that looks like a shoe. These long-legged, **wading** birds live in large swamps in eastern Africa. They are notable for staying still for a long time like statues. Just like storks, they are fairly tall and can grow up to *55 inches* in height.

African Fish Eagle

The *African fish eagle* lives in **sub-Saharan Africa**. They can be found near large bodies of water where they can catch fish. They can grow up to *30 inches* in length. They look like the *bald eagle,* which is the national bird of United States of America.

Spotted Eagle

The *spotted eagle* or *greater spotted eagle* is another African predatory bird. The lesser ones grow up to *24 inches* while greater spotted eagles can grow up to *28 inches*. These medium-sized eagles live in the north eastern parts of Africa. However, they are also known to breed in different places from time to time. They got their name from the white spots in their wings.

African Grey Hornbill

The *African grey hornbill* lives in sub-Saharan Africa. They can grow up to *18 inches* long. The feathers on their heads, tail, and wings have a darker color than the rest of their bodies. They also have a noticeable curved beak. They can grow up to *18 inches* in length.

Cut-Throat Finch

The *cut-throat finch* is a small bird that is common in Africa. They can grow around *4 inches* long. The male cut-throat finch is easily differentiated from the female because of a red pattern around their necks. The red color gets brighter as these birds grow older. Cut-throat finches often use the nests made by other birds.

African Penguin

There are some penguin species that do not live in cold places. The *African penguin* is an example of a penguin species that lives in southern Africa. They are known to make noises or *bray* like donkeys. They can grow up to *28 inches* when standing.

Cape Sugarbird

The *cape sugarbird* is common in the Western and Eastern capes of South Africa. Male cape sugarbirds have long tails and can grow up to *44 centimeters*. On the other hand, female cape sugarbirds have shorter tails and bills.

African Jacana

The *African jacana* is found in sub-Saharan Africa. They have long legs and claws that can help them walk over water plants in lakes where they look for insects to eat. This is why others call them *Jesus birds* because they look like they are walking on water. They are only about *30 centimeters long*.

Marabou Stork

The *marabou stork* is a wading bird that sometimes lives near humans in Africa. Although they are scavenging birds, they eat frogs, insects, fishes, and other small animals during the breeding season. They have very long legs and black wings that look like a cloak. They can grow quite big; up to *60* inches tall.

Southern Red Bishop

The *southern red bishop* is a small bird that can be found in the **wetlands** and grasslands of Africa. The males have bright red-orange and black feathers while females are brownish. They are only around *11 centimeters* long.

Northern Red Bishop

Although the *Northern Red Bishop* look similar to the Southern Red Bishop and in the past, the *northern red bishop* was known as a subspecies of the southern red bishop, these two species are completely different. The northern red bishops are bigger at around *15 centimeters*.

Lilac-breasted Roller

The *lilac-breasted roller* is a colorful bird that is common in sub-Saharan Africa. They go to high places such as poles and trees to find insects, snails, and lizards to eat. Despite their harmless look, they sometimes eat smaller birds. These birds grow up to *15 inches* in length. They are considered as a symbol of peace in Africa because of their beautiful colors.

African Paradise Flycatcher

The *African paradise flycatcher* is a bird that lives in sub-Saharan Africa near forests and the savanna. They only grow up to *17 centimeters* long, but males have a long tail. These birds are known to be noisy. Just like some other birds, male African paradise catchers have brighter colors than females.

Southern Masked Weaver

The *southern masked weaver* is a small bird that can be found in South Africa. They can be found in different habitats such as savannas, woodlands, wetlands, and grasslands. They can grow up to *14.5 centimeters* long. Male masked weavers are popular for their black masks and bright, yellow color.

Jackal Buzzard

The *jackal buzzard* is a predatory bird that lives in the savanna and grassland parts of South Africa. They can be found near **mountainous** regions. They hunt snakes, birds, insects, and other small animals for food. They can grow up to *55 centimeters long.*

African Sacred Ibis

The *African sacred ibis* is a wading bird that lives and breeds in sub-Saharan Africa. They can be found in the **mudflats** and wetlands where they hunt fish, insects, smaller birds, and frogs for food. This long-billed bird is the symbol of the Egyptian god *Thoth*. Their bodies can grow up to *27 inches* long.

African Grey Parrot

The *African grey parrot* is a species of highly intelligent parrots from Congo, Africa. They can learn to speak like humans and sometimes even follow orders. Scientists believe that they can be as smart as children between 4 and 6 years old. They mostly eat fruits, nuts, flowers, leaves, and **barks**. Sometimes, they also eat insects. They can grow up to *14 inches* in length.

Rufous-Naped Lark

The *rufous-naped lark* found in sub-Sahara Africa has a lot of **subspecies.** Most adult rufous-naped larks have crests on top of their heads. They feed on seeds, insects, and other **invertebrates**. These small birds can grow to around *18 centimeters* in length.

Pied Kingfisher

The *pied kingfisher* is a small bird that can be found in Africa and Asia. These crested birds can be seen **hovering** over lakes and rivers when they hunt for fish. When they see one, they dive down to catch it with their pointed beaks. They can grow up to *17 centimeters* long.

East African Crowned Crane

The *east African crowned crane,* a subspecies of the *grey crowned crane,* is a tall bird that can be found in Africa. They live in wetlands near rivers and lakes. These birds are special because they *dance* when attracting a mate. They would jump around and bow their heads.

White-Rumped Helmet Shrike

The *white-rumped helmet shrike* or just *white-rumped shrike* is a small bird that lives in eastern Africa. They live in the woodlands where they hunt for insects and fruits on the ground. Sometimes, they eat the insects crawling on the back of bigger animals. They can grow up to *23 centimeters* long. They get their name from the white *crowns* and rounded heads, which look like helmets.

African Hoopoe

The *hoopoe* is a medium-sized bird that can be found in many parts of the world, including Africa. Hoopoes in other countries tend to migrate, but those in Africa do not. They have crests with black markings on top of their brown heads. They can grow up to *32 centimeters* long.

Red-Necked Spurfowl

The *red-necked spurfowl* or *francolin* is a bird that lives in central Africa. They are cousins of the **domesticated** chicken. These birds move slowly and like to hide. Why? This is because they are hunted by human hunters as **game.** The largest red-necked spurfowl can grow up to *38 centimeters* long.

Woodland Kingfisher

The *woodland kingfisher* looks a lot different than the pied kingfisher. They live in the woodlands where they protect their territory from other birds by attacking them. These birds are colorful with a red upper bill and black wings with some light blue feathers. They can grow up to *23 centimeters* long.

Secretary Bird

The *secretary bird* is a strange bird with very long legs. They look like eagles with the long legs of a crane. These predatory birds use their powerful legs to attack their prey. They eat snakes, lizards, crabs, small birds, mice, hares, tortoises, and even bird eggs. Secretary birds are very big and can grow up to *4 feet* tall. Males have longer tail feathers and head **plumes.**

Fischer's Lovebird

The *Fischer's lovebird* is a small bird that is native to Africa. They are named after *Gustav Fischer,* a famous German explorer. The bright colors and small size of these birds have made them popular as house pets. They are intelligent and very friendly to humans. They eat mostly fruits and seeds. Fischer's lovebirds can grow up to *14 centimeters* long.

Grey-headed Kingfisher

The *grey-headed kingfishers* of South Africa looks a little like wooden kingfishers. They get their name from the grey color on top of their heads. Despite this, the rest of their bodies have bright colors. Even though they are kingfishers, they eat mostly small lizards and insects. These birds can grow up to *22 centimeters* long.

Kori Bustard

The *kori bustard* is a large bird that lives in South Africa. They can be found in grasslands, savannas, and **semi-deserts.** These birds are **omnivores.** They eat seeds, berries, flowers, plant roots, lizards, insects, and small mammals. Sometimes, they eat dead animals. They can grow up to *4 feet* and *11 inches* long.

African Bird Fun Facts

Africa is known to have one of the most **diverse** species of birds in the world. This means there are more species of birds in Africa than other places. Here are more *fun facts* that you didn't know about birds!

The Color of Flamingos

The natural pink dye that flamingos get from blue-green algae and brine shrimp is called *canthaxanthin*. If you don't think that you are what you eat, go ahead and ask a flamingo.

Standing on One Leg

Flamingos are very odd birds. While they have two long legs, they like to stand on *one leg*. They even sleep that way. Why? Scientists have no final answer right now. Some say they do this to preserve body heat in cold waters, but they also do this even in warm waters. No one has solved this mystery.

The Ostrich Egg

The egg of an ostrich is the biggest in the world today. They are also very strong. A human person can even stand on top of it without breaking. Since an adult ostrich is very heavy, their eggs are strong so they can sit on top of them and **incubate** them.

Bad Mating Habits

The male kori bustard attracts mates by making their throats look bigger. Male kori bustards are also known to attract many mates one after the other, so they are not exactly loyal.

Birds under the Sun

There are some birds that are **iridescent.** These birds appear to change color in different angles. One example is a sunbird which can be found in Africa as well as several other countries.

Smart Bird

While a lot of parrot species can only learn 50 words, the African grey parrot can learn around *800!* It is the most talkative bird on earth and one of the smartest birds on the planet!

Teamwork!

There are many bird species that are known to help each other. An example is how social weavers build a big nest for other birds of the same species, but they also tend to help birds of other species. Another example would be the *honeyguide* or *indicator bird* which is known to help humans find honey. They do this so they can eat the wax and **larvae** once the honey is collected. A lot of people also believe that they help other animals such as the *honey badger* find honey, but there is not enough evidence for this.

Learning Highlights: 10 Questions

The world of birds can be strange, but it is also an amazing place to explore. There are millions of things you can learn from birds. Sadly, not all of them can fit in this book. In fact, you have barely scratched the surface! Still, you should have learned many cool things about birds with this book. To highlight what you have learned, here are 10 questions about birds!

Question 1: Can all birds fly?

Answer: No. Some birds, like the ostrich, are too heavy to fly. Some birds can *glide,* but cannot fly longer distances.

Question 2: What do you call the mouths of birds?

Answer: Beaks or bills.

Question 3: Do all birds build and live in nests?

Answer: No. Some birds lay eggs and live in or on other places. Some birds lay eggs on the ground and in tree holes.

Question 3: Do birds live alone after leaving the nest?

Answer: Some birds may be alone or *solitary,* but a lot of bird species live in flocks.

Question 4: Is the ostrich the biggest bird that ever lived?

Answer: No. The biggest flying bird ever known is the *Pelagornis sandersi*, which is now extinct.

Question 5: Does Africa have the most species of birds?

Answer: Yes. The African continent has the highest diversity of bird species.

Question 6: Can birds of the same species have different colors?

Answer: Yes. A lot of bird species have different colors; mostly for different genders.

Question 7: If birds can fly in air and walk on land, can they swim in water?

Answer: Yes. African penguins as well as other penguin species can swim underwater. Some kingfishers can also dive through the water.

Question 8: Do birds eat other birds?

Answer: Yes. Many predatory birds eat smaller birds.

Question 9: Do birds fight other birds only for food?

Answer: No. A lot of birds, like the woodland kingfisher attack other birds to protect their territory. Birds like the fork-tailed drongo also attack other birds for self-defense.

Question 10: Does it always take a long time before birds can change colors?

Answer: *No.* While birds often change color seasonally or as they growing, other birds look iridescent when viewed from different angles.

Glossary

Archaeopteryx – The first known bird that lived 150 million years ago.

Camouflage – Blending with the color and appearance of the surroundings.

Crests – The spiky formation of feathers on top of a bird's head.

Diverse – Meaning many varieties.

Domesticated – Tamed and cultivated by humans for many purposes.

Endangered – Being in danger of going extinct (all members of the species dying).

Flightless – Cannot fly.

Flock – A group of birds or other animals.

Game – Animal being killed by human hunters for sports.

Hovering – Stay in one spot while flying.

Incubate – (Birds) Sitting on top of eggs to keep them warm.

Invertebrates – Animals without a vertebral column or *spine*.

Iridescent – Bright colors that look different from different angles.

Larvae/Larva – A young insect that will still change into an adult. This is called *metamorphosis.*

Migration – The movement of a species to another geographical location.

Mountainous – Near or around mountains.

Omnivores – Can eat meat as well as plant foods.

Plumage – The feathers of birds.

Plume – A part of the plumage.

Predatory – Animals or birds that eat meat by killing other animals.

Scavenging – Eating the leftover meat of dead animals.

Semi-desert – An area between a desert and a grassland or woodland.

Sub-Saharan – The area south of the Saharan desert in Africa.

Subspecies – Related to or a member of a bigger species.

Territory – An area being protected or dominated.

Thermal Lift – The upward force made by rising hot air.

Wading – Moving or walking through water.

Wetlands – An area where the land is soaked with water for long periods; sometimes permanently.

Wingspan – The length of a bird's wings when extended.

Conclusion

Thank you again for downloading this book!

I hope you enjoyed reading about my book on the birds of Africa!

Remember that there are thousands of other bird species out there to read about! If you are interested in knowing more about birds, you can soar to your local bookstore, search the amazing World Wide Web or your nearest library or better yet plan a trip to see these birds in real life. Maybe not today or tomorrow, but in your *future!*

Finally, if you enjoyed this book, please take the time to share your thoughts and **post a review on Amazon**. It would be greatly appreciated!

Thank you!

A Note About The Author:

Sean Liburd is a father, husband, entrepreneur, community builder, educator, listener and thinker. He is the founder and co-owner of Knowledge Bookstore which was established on December 18, 1997. Sean has learned that books educate and inform - but they also make you laugh, wonder and carry you to worlds you've never heard of inhabited by people you've never seen - a kaleidoscope of cultures painted on the pages in words, in pictures and in dreams. Books "Awaken the Mind" which is both Knowledge Bookstore's slogan and Sean's goal.

Feel free to contact Sean Liburd at azlpublishing@gmail.com www.knowledgebookstore.com

Next Steps

- Write me an honest review about the book – I truly value your opinion and thoughts and I will incorporate them into my next book, which is already underway.

Check Out My Other Books

Go ahead and click on the links below to check out the other great books I've published!

Butterflies and Moths:: All about Butterflies and Moths, a Kids Introduction to Butterflies and Moths-Fun Facts and Fantastic Photos!

African Elephants Fun Facts and Fantastic Photos for Kids!: Learn About African Animals

Awaken the Mind: Communion with Sean Liburd

www.ingramcontent.com/pod-product-compliance
Lightning Source LLC
Chambersburg PA
CBHW050821290526
45792CB00001B/211